that all may be
ONE

Association of Colleges of Sisters of St. Joseph

Martha Malinski, Editor

Printed in the United States of America
First Printing, 2019
ISBN: 978-1-54398-920-5
www.acssj.org

Cover Illustration Copyright © Julie Lonneman
Cover design, book design and production by Mary Sommerhauser

Unifying Love

Carol Allan, SSJ

God, known by many names,

The Sisters of St. Joseph were founded
    to be the Congregations of the "great love of God"
    recognizing You and our neighbor
    in the breaking of the bread.

They respond freely and joyously
    to the call of the Spirit
    to love God, the dear neighbor and all creation.

Their dedication to serving the neighbor
    with preference to the poor
    has been their hallmark through the centuries.

In union with You who is the origin of all,
    they seek in all things what is most loving.
In union with the Word of God,
    they empty themselves
    for the sake of the other.
In union with the Spirit,
    they realize and express
    God's love in the world.

This is the gift that was given to the Sisters,
    who embraced Your people and now share
    their heritage and charism with all.

We pray that like the Sisters of St. Joseph
    we carry the torch of their charism of
    uniting neighbor with neighbor and
    neighbor with God without distinction,
    until all may be one.

Amen

Table of Contents

Introduction

Martha Malinski, Editor & Executive Director

This book is designed to provide a historical overview, and a contemporary expression of the spiritual tradition and charism of the Sisters of St. Joseph. The book is divided into different sections: history, spiritual practices, prayers, and maxims. Read the book from front to back or dive into a section that speaks to you. The authors hope to inspire you and ignite the spirit of the Sisters of St. Joseph in your daily life.

This publication is produced by the Association of Colleges of Sisters of St. Joseph. The Association of Colleges of Sisters of St. Joseph draws together nine colleges and universities founded by the Sisters of St. Joseph to articulate and further the contemporary expression of the educational mission and legacy of the Sisters of St. Joseph. The Association fosters collaboration among all the member institutions, provides resources for faculty, staff and students at the member colleges and universities, and encourages mission integration on each campus.

All member institutions in the Association of Colleges of Sisters of St. Joseph hold values in common. These include:

- Creating hospitable and caring campus communities
- Manifesting concern for all without distinction
- Addressing the needs of the times
- Striving for excellence in all endeavors
- Working to make a difference in the local and world community

For more information and resources, visit our website at: www.acssj.org.

ACSSJ Member Institutions and Founding Dates

1905

St. Catherine University
St. Paul, Minnesota

1916

Avila University
Kansas City, Missouri

1916

St. Joseph's College
Brooklyn & Patchogue, New York

1920

The College of Saint Rose
Albany, New York

1923

Fontbonne University
St. Louis, Missouri

1924

Chestnut Hill College
Philadelphia, Pennsylvania

1925

Mount Saint Mary's University
Los Angeles, California

1927

Regis College
Weston, Massachusetts

1928

College of Our Lady of the Elms
Chicopee, Massachusetts

Lace

Carol Allan, SSJ and Martha Malinski

For the Sisters of St. Joseph, lace holds both a historical and a symbolic significance.

In the mid-to-late 1600s in Europe, everyone demanded lace, especially royalty. The city of Le Puy, France, home for the first Sisters of St. Joseph, was renowned for its exquisite bobbin lace. The sisters earned their livelihood by making lace and teaching women the art of bobbin lace-making. These sisters provided the women with a skill they could use to earn a living with dignity. Additionally, the act of weaving lace may have provided the sisters and other women the opportunity to share the deepest desires of their hearts. At other times, the repetitive experience of creating lace could form a background for contemplative prayer.

Lace threads symbolize the relational call of the Sisters of St. Joseph, the call to unifying love that unites neighbor with neighbor, and neighbor with God, without distinction. The spaces in the lace threads signify brokenness and oppression. These spaces also show an openness to the Spirit who lives among all creation.

Throughout this book, threads of lace are visible. These images help to connect past and future together, creating a piece that binds humanity together while remaining open for a new design. The lace-making that began in 1650 is not completed. Our hands now hold these threads. We are the weavers. We are asked to carry the legacy forward, designing, creating and sending forth blessings to our world.

History
of the Sisters of St. Joseph

Shannon Green and Mary Sommerhauser

The Sisters of St. Joseph were founded in 1650 in the small city of Le Puy-en-Velay, located in the Haute-Loire Department of south-central France. Le Puy-en-Velay translates to "the needle in the valley." These needles are pillars of volcanic rock as seen in the image below. This unique geography has drawn travelers and settlers to Le Puy since its establishment in the Third Century. Atop one needle is the Rocher Saint-Michel d'Aiguilhe, a chapel dedicated to the Archangel (right). It was built in 961 and the first Sisters of St. Joseph likely prayed there. Another needle is the site of Notre-Dame de France (left). This statue of the Virgin Mary was built in 1860, constructed out of the metal of 213 cannons used in the Crimean War. The historic Cathedral Notre-Dame du Puy towers over the town atop another volcanic pillar (middle steeple). The Cathedral's construction began in the 11th Century and since then has served as a starting point for pilgrims on the Camino de Santiago, the Way of St. James. Pilgrims still gather daily at the morning Mass to receive their blessing before beginning the nearly 750 kilometer walk to Santiago de Compostela in Spain.

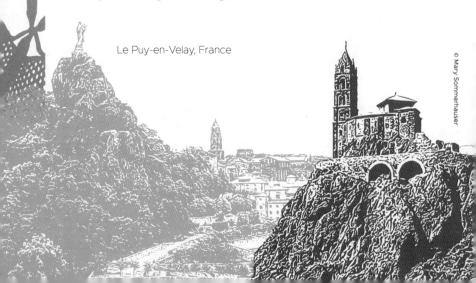

Le Puy-en-Velay, France

Founders' Prayer

Joan Lescinski, CSJ & Katherine Hanley, CSJ

Loving God, we thank you for your many gifts, especially
for the gift of time to come together to reflect and to plan;
we ask you to bless this time together.

In the companionship of our patron, St. Joseph, we gather
in the spirit of our founding Sisters. Give us their
eagerness to educate others in your ways, their generosity
to serve others and their courage to risk the familiar to
reach out to the wider world.

Françoise (a-road) Eyraud
Anna (fay) Vey
Anna Brun
Marguerite (Birdie-a) Burdier
Anna (Cha-lay) Chaleyer
Clauda Chastel

In the names of the foremothers, in the name of all those
who have gone before us, and in the
name of those who bring their presence to life,
we ask your blessing.

Amen.

Our Foundations

Shannon Green

The history of the Sisters of St. Joseph begins more than 350 years ago in the medieval city of Le Puy-en-Velay, France, where a small group of women gathered together with a desire to serve their "dear neighbor." The recent Wars of Religion had devastated France resulting in at least three million deaths. Many men did not return home to Le Puy from battle. Their families were left in poverty with little means of survival. Famine and pestilence drove rural farmers to the city searching for work, and the plague was rampant. In 1650, Le Puy was in the midst of great instability, violence, and destitution.

Six women named Françoise Eyraud, Anna Vey, Anna Brun, Marguerite Burdier, Anna Chaleÿer and Clauda Chastel, saw this suffering and, as women of deep faith, felt called to respond. Dressed as widows, they "divided the city" going out to every quarter of Le Puy to ask the people what they needed. In response to these needs, the women ministered to the sick, the poor, widows, and orphans, living out the works of mercy. In the evenings, they gathered in their kitchen (pictured on the right) where they would receive those in need, and likely shared their daily experience of serving their neighbors. As women of prayer, the Sisters of St. Joseph continue to gather together to nourish their spiritual and communal lives with a prayer practice we now know as "sharing the state of the heart."

The sisters went about their ministry quietly and unnoticed because service to the community as single women was unheard of, and unacceptable at that time. Women who desired a religious life would enter the convent as a nun and live a life of prayer and study behind convent walls. These six women wanted to live out their faith by serving their neighbors while living in the world, not inside a cloister.

These women found support and guidance in a Jesuit priest, Father Jean-Pierre Médaille. Fr. Médaille was an itinerant preacher who

Illustration based on the first kitchen of the Sisters of St. Joseph in Le Puy-en-Velay

© Carol Hebert, SSJ

> 66 **They shall practice all the spiritual and corporal works of mercy of which women are capable, and that will most benefit the dear neighbor."**

met them in the small towns around Le Puy. He heard in them the desire to address the needs of the community, so he helped the women gather together, and offered them spiritual direction and religious education. Only two of the sisters could read and write, so Father Médaille wrote one hundred Maxims for them to memorize, and composed their earliest Constitutions, where he wrote, "They shall practice all the spiritual and corporal works of mercy of which women are capable, and that will most benefit the dear neighbor." The local bishop, Henri de Maupas, was supportive of the women and in 1650 sponsored their association; within a few years the Sisters of St. Joseph received recognition from the Church. The Sisters of St. Joseph are among the earliest communities of sisters in church history with an "apostolic" mission, that is, active service to the community outside the cloister walls.

In this era, there were few ways women could support themselves, and the devastation of the war left many women and children in dire poverty. Some had to resort to prostitution or other forms of exploitation in order to survive. The Sisters of St. Joseph wanted to provide these women with greater dignity by teaching them a skill they could use to earn a living. The sisters taught women and girls to make cotton lace, which was in great demand at the time. Using this skill, they could earn a living and provide for their families.

Over the next 100 years, more than 150 communities of Sisters of St. Joseph were established across France.

In 1789, France entered the tumultuous period of the French Revolution, whose participants sought to confront the corrupt power structures of France. The hierarchy of the Catholic Church was closely aligned with the monarchy and was therefore a target of the revolutionists. While religious communities like the Sisters of St. Joseph were not in positions of power, they too were swept up in the climate of the Revolution and were suppressed by the new government. The sisters, like all religious communities, were pressured to take a constitutional oath to the state, which would place their loyalties above the Church. Sisters and priests who refused to take the oath were forced out of ministry and risked imprisonment.

Mother St. John Fontbonne was a young and gifted superior of the Sisters of St. Joseph in Monistrol-sur-Loire, not far from Le Puy. Taking the constitutional oath was unthinkable to Mother St. John, and she refused repeatedly despite constant pressure from the local priest. Her fellow sisters followed her lead, and they continued to serve in their hospital and school in Monistrol until they were expelled in 1793. She returned to her family home in Bas-en-Basset, but in 1794, she was imprisoned with four other sisters, including her sibling Marie, and her aunt, both Sisters of St. Joseph, and given a date for execution. In fact, five sisters of St. Joseph were beheaded at the guillotine during the French Revolution for this refusal to pledge loyalty to the state.

The night before the scheduled execution of Mother St. John and her sisters, political leader Maximilien Robespierre, who orchestrated this "reign of terror," was overthrown. Instead of going to the guillotine, the sisters were set free. However, they could not return to their convent or their ministries.

Mother St. John returned to her family home in Bas-en-Basset for several years. She cared for her parents, nieces and nephews, and eventually provided religious education in the local parish. She lived her religious life quietly and as faithfully as she could within the confines of her home.

Over the next decade, the Catholic Church and religious orders were allowed to reopen their churches and convents throughout France. In 1807, Father Claude Cholleton of Saint-Étienne began to guide a group of women known as the "Black Daughters" who desired to be sisters. Father Cholleton felt that their way of life was too strict; he also saw the potential for these women to serve those in need in the community. After consulting with Cardinal Fesch of Lyon, Father Cholleton asked Mother St. John to come to Saint-Étienne and use her gifts of leadership to form these women in religious life. It was a difficult decision for her as she was very close to her family, especially after all they experienced during the Revolution. Mother St. John found the courage to accept this invitation and she went to Saint-Étienne to assume leadership of this fledgling group. In 1808, they took the habit of the Sisters of St. Joseph, joining the rebirth of the communities of women religious around France. The priest said in his homily, "You my dear daughters are few in numbers, but like a swarm of bees, you will spread everywhere. Your numbers shall be as the stars of heaven." (Saravia 2008, 27)

By 1816, the Sisters of St. Joseph had outgrown their quarters in Saint-Étienne, so Mother St. John established the motherhouse in Lyon. She was re-elected by her sisters to lead the congregation for more than thirty years and was finally allowed to retire in 1839. Under Mother St. John's leadership, the sisters grew to over 200

> **❝** You my dear daughters are few in numbers, but like a swarm of bees, you will spread everywhere. Your numbers shall be as the stars of heaven.**"**

foundations across France. She died in 1843, nearly 50 years after her imprisonment and near execution.

Prior to her retirement, Mother St. John's courage and vision led to an even greater expansion of the Sisters of St. Joseph to the United States. In 1834, having heard of the good work of the Sisters of St. Joseph, Bishop Joseph Rosati of St. Louis, Missouri wrote to Mother St. John to ask for sisters to be sent to open a school for poor children. Six sisters volunteered to embark on this mission, including two of Mother St. John's nieces. In 1836, they left the comfort of the modern city of Lyon and boarded an ocean liner to cross the Atlantic. Most of them would never return home to France. These first sisters were Febronie Fontbonne, St. Protais Débiolle, Febronie Chapellon, Delphine Fontbonne, Philomène Vilaine, and Marguerite-Félicité Bouté. Later, Celestine Pommerel and Julie Fournier joined them.

The sisters arrived in a small town outside St. Louis, named Carondelet, and opened schools for many underserved communities, including the poor and children of freed slaves. They also opened an Institute for the Deaf, which continues to serve the deaf community today. Mother St. John kept in touch with her sisters through letters, offering her love, gratitude and support to them. Many of the Sisters of St. Joseph in North America trace their beginnings to the foundation in St. Louis. From St. Louis, sisters branched out throughout the United States and Canada, establishing new communities, and opening ministries, including colleges and universities, that continue to serve the dear neighbor.

Streets of Le Puy

Mary Catherine Walton, SSJ

Who has walked upon these cobblestones?
Whose feet have left impressions,
Felt in lingering energies of deeds done here?
Whose feet left imprints of agonies and miseries and joys,
That remains in memory and fact?
Holy ones,
Soldiers, revolutionists, and poor folk
Have trod the streets that are still here—though they are gone.
The yesterdays call us to remember
Those who birthed us here.
With gratitude, we bow our hearts
To the inheritance of love
They have left for us to grow in and grow into.
This path has voice in the choice some women made long ago.
Now the path they took stretches across the earth.
And we walk in their footsteps.

Spirit and Charism
of the Sisters of St. Joseph

Carol Allan, SSJ

The Spirit and Charism of the Sisters of St. Joseph calls us to unifying love with God and with all people. This communion is within each of us, advancing our relationship with God, our "dear neighbor," and all of creation. The Sisters of St. Joseph's spirituality challenges us to think with magnanimous hearts, with expansive souls, and with noble minds: Our love for God is to be "generous, embracing all that love is capable of and all that a heart can love in God and for God" (Maxims of Perfection 9:2). The charism informs us of how we interact within creation, uniting neighbor with neighbor, and neighbor with God, without distinction, so that all may be one.

The charism is the essence of the Sisters of St. Joseph, calling forth a relationship with God, our neighbor, with others, and all of creation.

Everyone who embraces the charism is empowered in unifying love with God and all creation until we are united as one.

© Mary Sommerhauser

Stained glass window at the Mother House chapel in Lyon, France. The lily flower is symbolic of St. Joseph.

Consensus Statement of the Central Ideas

of Jean-Pierre Médaille, SJ,

Found in the Primitive Constitutions

Stimulated by the Holy Spirit of Love
and receptive to inspiration

we move always towards profound love of God and
love of neighbor without distinction
from whom we do not separate ourselves and
for whom, in the following of Christ
we work in order to achieve unity
of neighbor with neighbor
and neighbor with God
directly in this apostolate and
indirectly through works of charity
in humility — the spirit of the Incarnate Word,
(Philippians 2:5-11)

in sincere charity (cordiale charité)
— the manner of Saint Joseph whose name we bear

in an Ignatian-Salesian climate:
that is, with an orientation towards excellence
(Le dépassement, le plus)
tempered by gentleness (douceur), peace, joy.

Based on the central ideas of Father Jean-Pierre Médaille, SJ, found in the primitive constitutions, and as researched and adapted from the US Federation of Sisters of St. Joseph. (United States Federation of Sisters of St. Joseph - http://www.cssjfed.org/about-us)

Portrait of a "Daughter of St. Joseph"

Father Marius Nepper, SJ

Eyes open
on a world both miserable and sinful,
but a world worked on by the Holy Spirit;

Eyes open and ears attentive
to the sufferings of the world;

Eyes open, ears attentive and spirit alert,
never settled down, always in a holy disquietude,
searching…in order to understand
to divine what God
and the dear neighbor await from her
today, now, for the body and for the soul;

**Eyes open, ears attentive, spirit alert…
sleeves rolled up for ministry,**
without excluding
the more humble, the less pleasing,
the less noticeable;

Finally, in her face the reflection of the virtue
proper to our Congregation,
"continual joy of spirit."

This is the quiet inner glow
of the Sister whose life in the service of Jesus Christ
has been successful.

Ready to Respond

Joannie Cassidy, SSJ

Embraced by the circle of Divine Love
I am enfolded by the Women of Le Puy
Women of rock and fire
Infusing Passion, Purpose and
their Porous hearts into my own

Grounded in Grace, the embers flame once again
Their yes breathes life into my yes...

From the center... the circle widens and I move to the margins
trusting the testimony of this Holy Ground
The Clarion Call awaits
May I... May We... be ready to respond.

Prayer in the Spirit of Mother St. John Fontbonne

Author Unknown

God of wisdom and grace,
we pray in the spirit of Mother St. John Fontbonne.
May our lives model her humility, fidelity and courage
as we embrace this present moment.
With an expansive heart,
Mother St. John Fontbonne opened herself
to the unfolding mystery of God's call
in herself and in the dear neighbor.
Inspired by her vision, strength, and compassion,
may we live and work
with the Zeal of Christ Jesus, "that all may be one."
Amen.

© Julie Lonneman

Mother St. John Fontbonne

Sharing the State of the Heart

Compiled by Lori Helfrich

Introduction

Lori Helfrich

Sharing the State of the Heart is a unique spiritual practice of the Sisters of St. Joseph. It has endured since the first sisters gathered in the kitchen in Le Puy, France. Inspired by Fr. Jean-Pierre Médaille, SJ, their spiritual director, and guide, Sharing the State of the Heart emerges from the Ignatian spirituality of finding God in all things. Sharing the State of the Heart inspires people to look at ordinary life events and see the deeper spiritual meaning that reveals God through those everyday occurrences.

Sharing the State of the Heart and Order of the House is a communal practice and can be modified for various groups. The following pages offer an outline beginning with a gathering prayer, individual reflection, followed by communal sharing and ending with a closing prayer. The Sharing the State of the Heart begins with individuals reflecting on what is stirring in their hearts. After self-reflection, participants begin to share with others their order of the house. Then the practice continues to shift outward to reflect communally on how God, the Holy Spirit, is moving among them.

Sharing State of the Heart and Order of the House continues the deep rooted tradition of the Sisters of St. Joseph into the present time and reaches out to people who embrace the spirit and charism. It draws all those in the family of Joseph together in unity so that all may be one.

Gathering Prayer

Suzanne Franck, CSJ

God of all creation, you surround us and dwell within us.
We are grateful for this time of joining with others
to share our prayer and our reflections.

May your Spirit of Wisdom inspire us to open our eyes to see as you see,
open our ears to hear more deeply than the words spoken,
open our heart to touch the heart of others.

May your Spirit of Love give us courage to build relationships that
empower us, so together we bring unioning love to our world.

With St. Joseph as our example, may we continue to trust in God
and be faithful to all that God calls us to be, as we journey together
into our future.

We ask this in Jesus' name.
Amen.

Sharing the State of the Heart Continued

Use the reflection questions below to focus on this prayer practice.

State of the Heart

- How do I come today? How is my heart?
- Is there anything stirring in my prayer or in my life that I want to express?
- Where did I see God today, in the people, in the work, in prayer?
- What am I noticing about prayer?
  - About my relationship with God?
  - About my relationship with myself?
  - About my family? My community?
- How balanced or unbalanced has my life been?
  - Can I name a feeling stirring in my heart?

Order of the House

- Individually think:
  - How do we see God's love moving in these stories?
  - How do these stories reflect our responses to God's love?
  - How do we see God working in our lives?
  - What is moving in each of us as we listen to our reflections?
  - How are our hearts being moved, challenged, inspired, drawn?
- Community then asks:
  - What do we look like as a group?
  - What seems to be coming together for us?
  - What is opening up as possibility? How do we respond?
  - What symbol or image represents God's action in us?

Closing Prayer
Intuition of the Heart
Modified from a prayer by Katherine Hanley, CSJ & Kathy Sherman, CSJ

God of all, you speak to us continually through the marvels of your creation and through the secret movements of our own hearts.

We are grateful for the opportunity to join with others who work to create a better world for all.

With St. Joseph as our example and guide, help us to deepen our listening hearts so that we may hear clearly your Holy Spirit speaking within; and give us the strength to believe in and respond to your love.

Enflame our hearts with the fire of your love that we may build bonds of relationship and respect among all sharing in unioning love.

Help our hearts of stone become hearts of flesh.

That we may encounter and journey with those we meet during our time here.

We ask this in the name of the Most Holy Trinity.

Amen.

Femme Fontbonne

Sisters of St. Joseph of Lyon

Vallée du Velay :
>   Rivières de vie,
>   Collines d'espérance.

Cité du Puy :
>   Tours solides,
>   Toits d'amour.

Famille des Fontbonne :
>   Fontaine de foi,
>   Fontaine de bonne eau.

Ville de Lyon :
>   Source de nouvelle naissance,
>   Graines d' engagement.

Mère St. Jean :
>   Puits de sagesse
>   Source de courage.

Soeurs et Collaborateurs St. Joseph :
>   Semeurs de renouveau,
>   Chemins de la Parole!

Fontbonne Woman

Velay Valley:
> Rivers of life,
> Hills of hope.

City of Le Puy:
> Towers of strength,
> Rooftops of love.

Family of Fontbonne:
> Fountain of faith,
> Fountain of good water.

City of Lyon:
> Source of new birth,
> Seeds of commitment.

Mother St. John:
> Well of wisdom
> Source of courage.

St. Joseph Sisters and Co-Partners:
> Sowers of renewal,
> Paths of the Word!

Prayers and Reflections

Carol Allan, SSJ and Sean Peters, CSJ

Prayer forms the backbone of the life and ministry of a Sister of St. Joseph. In prayer, each person comes to know God and her own deepest spirit and unites herself with God, with neighbor and with all creation.

The prayers offered in this section and throughout this book come from a variety of sources, but all embody the spirit and charism of the Sisters of St. Joseph. They also include prayers focused on our patron, St. Joseph.

Sit quietly with some of these prayers, allow them to speak in and through you. You can also use the prayers in this book for communal prayer, for example, at the beginning of a meeting or some other gathering. In a group setting, feel free to change the pronouns in the prayers from the singular to the plural.

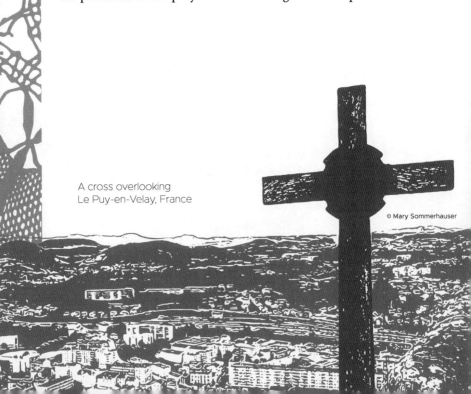

A cross overlooking
Le Puy-en-Velay, France

© Mary Sommerhauser

Learning to Pray

Christine Parks, CSJ

I used to pray for God to change the world.
I used to pray for God to change others.
I used to pray for God to change.

I used to pray to a God of magical miracles.
Prayed for small miracles
Like passing tests I hadn't studied for
Like no rain for our picnic—even though
     farmers were desperate for rain.

I didn't pray for big ones like
     burning bushes,
          multiplying loaves and fish,
               water into wine,
                    lepers cured and demons cast out.

Though I did pray for world peace more than once.

Small miracles were mostly what I wanted—until the day
I met you on a hot summer hillside.
A day when the sky was such deep dark blue
     I could fall into it if I didn't hold on.
And there you were talking about love, being love,
     being in love...with me.

You taught me that the miracle was in me
that my prayer wasn't changing anyone else
     or the world,
it was changing me—into love
that was the miracle.
That would change the world.

St. Joseph Prayer

Adapted prayer by Kathy Sherman, CSJ

Teach us to listen and not be afraid
to trust as you did in God's promise.

Teach us to love courageously
with a heart that is free and just.

Teach us to protect one another
and all that belongs to God.

Teach us to dream a world where
all are neighbors; a vision
illumined by God's light.

Teach us to keep the Word of God
close to our hearts, and to proclaim
it in word and action.

Teach us to be gentle with our power
and strong in our tenderness.

Teach us to be for our children
a living lesson of goodness and truth
a blessing of hope for all generations
to come.

Teach us to live the charism of the
founders, the Sisters of St. Joseph of uniting neighbor with
neighbor and neighbor with God without distinction.

Amen.

Pilgrims All are We

Carol Allan, SSJ

God of our journey, we come as pilgrims.
We want to experience our beginnings and our history.

May we travel
with hearts open to the newness you offer us,
with eyes open to the beauty around us,
with hands open to one another in community.

Gracious God,
we carry with us
our beloved families and friends
our colleges and our colleagues
our dear neighbors all over the world.

Bless us with laughter and with learning.
Bless us with the ability to travel light.
Bless us with the spirit of our founders.

May we travel safely.
May we bring experiences back to our campus communities.
May we travel with you, God, this day and all of our days.
Amen.

Founders Prayer

Author Unknown

O God,
thank you for calling together
six women over 350 years ago—
six women who still serve as our Founders today.
Thank you for calling together
women and men in our day
to serve as examples for us—
examples of suffering with the poor,
of learning from those we serve,
of putting everything into life,
of stepping into new places,
and of uncovering the face of God.

O God,
teach us to imitate not their actions but their desire—
their desire to seek and to share your presence,
their desire to respond to a world in need,
their desire to love their sisters and brothers-
their dear neighbors.
And as we open our desires to your call,
lead us and guide us in your grace.
We offer our thanks and ask our prayer
in the name of Jesus,
who lives within us now and forever.
Amen.

Breathe

Joan Marie Gleason, CSJ

My God,
I breathe out my fear,
And breathe in your strength.

I breathe out my confusion
And breathe in your peace.

I breathe out my resentments
And breathe in your love.

I praise you with Every breath I take.

Joseph, Our Patron

Julie Harkins, CSJ

Loving God, I thank you and praise you for the power of your presence deep in our hearts, the vitality of your presence here in our midst, for this opportunity to pray and to celebrate our common hope.

Who is Joseph? There is the Joseph of our first six sisters, the Joseph of the early documents and our Joseph... the Joseph each and every one of us finds when we look deep into the common spiritual core of our shared identity with the Sisters of St. Joseph. Our Joseph is the Joseph of the loving manner: not so much the Joseph who served and ministered, as the Joseph who served and ministered lovingly, with care and concern; not so much the Joseph who did or who was this or that, as the Joseph whose actions and words and intentions and works were characterized by a manner that was loving and caring and concerned.

An Opening Prayer

Author Unknown
Adapted from Father Marius Nepper, SJ's description of a Sister of St. Joseph

We pray, that God bless us with
eyes open to the world,
the misery that exists and the Spirit that inspires.
That God bless us with
Ears attentive to the suffering and the joy
of the world and of our companions in ministry.
That God bless us with
a vigilant spirit, never settling down,
always with a holy restlessness, searching...
in order to understand, to divine
what God and the dear neighbor await from us
for the body and for the soul today.
That God bless us with
sleeves rolled up for service,
without excluding the most humble,
the less pleasing, the least noticeable.
That God bless us with the grace to
reflect in our faces continual joy of spirit.
We ask this in Jesus' name,
Amen.

Where Would We Be?

Mary Catherine Walton, SSJ

Where would we be
if six women had not taken the risk
to embrace a vision to effect change in even just one city,
one countryside,
one set of circumstances?
It took six women to multiply the grace,
to set the pace that traverses the world,
that has left footprints outside our door.

Where would we be
if they had walked away from the kitchen,
from the unknown,
from the challenge that God's Spirit asked them to choose?

What would be missing from our world
if the Revolution chaos
had crushed Médaille's dream into the dust,
if it had rusted the hopes that lived in Joseph's
house?

What might have happened
if Jeanne Fontbonne had not embraced the Black
Daughters as Sisters in Lyon?

What would now stand
in Le Puy, Lyon, Carondelet, Chestnut Hill and other places
if zealous women had stayed within the comfort zone of their culture,
afraid of the emotion of facing something new?

Do we not know the scent of death and dying—from our roots?
Do we not know the sounds of courage and risk
that echo through our history?
We are built upon transformation!

We have never just survived.
In hiddenness we have embraced Mystery
and
we can do it again!
It is our turn to set the pace into tomorrow.

St. Joseph, Help Us in Our Work

Sean Peters, CSJ

St. Joseph, our patron and guide, you worked as a carpenter which called for creativity, resourcefulness, steadfastness and strength.

Our work demands these same virtues. So we ask for

the creativity to see beyond our present reality,

the resourcefulness to use the many gifts God provides,

the steadfastness to stay with the tasks set before us and

the strength to meet the challenges that come along the way.

And may we ask for one more gift that you experienced—to be delighted by the presence of Jesus in the midst of our busy days.

We ask this in Jesus' name.

Amen.

Thank You for the Gift of Today

Pat Bergen, CSJ

Gracious God,

Thank you for the gift of today.

Refresh me... Invite me...

To discover your presence in each person

That I meet and every event encountered.

Teach me when to speak, when to listen.

When to ponder and when to share.

In moments of challenge and decision

Attune my heart to the whisperings

Of your Wisdom.

As I undertake ordinary and unnoticed tasks, gift me with simple joy.

When my day goes well, may I rejoice!

When it grows difficult,

Surprise me with new possibilities.

When life is overwhelming

Call me to Sabbath moments

To restore your peace and harmony.

May my living today

Reveal your goodness.

Amen.

What Do We Know by Heart?

Katherine Hanley, CSJ

We are the daughters and sons of women who knew the vision by heart.

They furnished a room in every religious community for the poor and the homeless because of that vision.

We are the daughters and sons of women who went to the guillotine for their vision-which they knew by heart.

We are the daughters and sons of women who crossed an ocean— two novices and four professed—for their vision.

We are the daughters and sons of women who learned a foreign language so they could live and minister to us—sent by a vision of hope.

We are the sisters and brothers of women who went, when they were 60 and 70, to start missions in foreign lands because of what they knew by heart.

We are the daughters and sons of a saint who fell madly and wildly in love and accepted his wife's mysterious pregnancy because he knew her by heart.

We have genes for passion.

We are the women and men who have stories and secrets and visions and dreams of incredible passion.

How can we not?

So how are we going to choose life?

And what sort of life are we going to choose?

We may discover that our touchstones are as simple and as disconcerting as the ones Scripture gives us.

And as passionate.

Let us pray for this gift for one another here and as we walk together toward a God who has already chosen to learn each one of us by heart.

Not Taken Alone

Joannie Cassidy, SSJ

Rekindling the fire of our founders,
each step exhaled the mystical knowing of memory
as I walked the pilgrim path.

The fidelity of their footsteps
prompts toward the *prochain*,
the dear neighbor in front of me.
Courage and zeal
Fuse into my foot bed
a pathway not taken alone.

Log cabin in Carondelet, Missouri that served as the first location in the United
States in 1836. The cabin was built in 1833 by the Sisters of Charity.

Kaleidoscope of the Little Design

Jane DeLisle, CSJ

A blend of light and ready hearts
Imagination captured
Love made manifest in the Little Design
God's pleading heard by a small group of women
Be love! Be joy! Be gentle presence!

A vocation so sublime
Mystical union
Love poured out
Spirit at work
Movements of grace
Love known in ready hearts given to God
Presence in the Little Design

A reflection of light
A movement of grace
Gifts given!
A broken world in need of healing and compassion
In poverty, deprivation, destitution
Love finds the way
The truth is realized:
God present in it all
Precisely in the need!
Shifting light reflects the image
Divide the City!
Listen! See! Together respond to ills!
The face of God revealed
In the weak, the vulnerable, in every human face

Then, an unsettling turn
Darkest night—
Revolution!
Love under siege
Arrested, imprisoned, suppressed
Life threatened and lost
One stands alone in the darkness

With faintest sleight of hand
The alteration of life's schemes and all its scopes
A new beginning across the sea
All with a turn of the kaleidoscope

Generation after generation
A shift of reality and circumstance
New beauty, new grace in response to the Mission
The amazing Little Design adapts
Alert to the next place for Love's revelation
The cry for unity and reconciliation

A kaleidoscope turns
New patterns emerge
Nothing is lost.

The color and reflection of today's Little Design
Fashioned anew in our times
Generous hearts awake to the needs of a new society
The Wonder of the Little Design

We Will Need Courage

Judy Lovchik, CSJ and Clare Dunn, CSJ

We will need courage,
    we will need energy,
        we will need vision,
we will need to be at ease with ourselves
        and our decisions.

Above all, like the psalmist,
    we will need to keep "our eyes
        fixed on the Lord, our God"
            until God has mercy on us,
                until God lets us rest.

And then we will know,
    as we have always known,
that the effort was worth the gift of our lives,
    the best of our years,
        the length of our days.
Amen.

A New Harvest

Alberta Cammack, CSJ

They had learned the total emptying of self
to be filled with God, these black-robed women
who carried their baskets to the poor, bathed the sick,
gently tended the wounded, and lovingly gathered together
the orphans in their outstretched arms.

Uncommon women for an uncommon time
they were not formed by formal rule
to be the congregation of the great love of God.
The world still needs their kind of loving.
With a new harvest the chaff is scattered by the wind.

Through different pathways women will come
with new voices taking up the singing.
They will come and listen to the unspoken,
walk in strange places, and dream strong dreams.

CSJ Charism Prayer

Joan Mitchell, CSJ ——————————————————

Let us roll up our sleeves
to do all of which women are capable
as we have from the beginning.

Let us divide the city
for the work of mercy
as we have from the beginning.

And partner with our neighbors,
local and global, for the work of justice
as we have from our beginning.

Let us weave community
in new and expanding patterns
of lace and grace
as we have from our beginning.

Stir our chaos into being, Spirit of God.
Hearten our struggles for inclusion.
Sustain our hopes for a just and holy world.

Complete the work you have begun in us.
Amen.

Weaving Inclusive Love

Joanne Gallagher, CSJ

God of inclusive love,
Enflame our hearts with the fire of your love
that we may build bonds of relationship and respect among all.

Our story springs from a small group of courageous women.
They were lace makers who wove a pattern of inclusive love
across France and across our world.

More than three and a half centuries later we continue to tell the story
of how this pattern continues to weave across our world.
Deepen our awareness that our work is a ministry
that weaves the story of inclusive love
throughout the neighborhood of the universe.

May the sacred threads of this story impel us to action —
action that stirs up love in our world
and calls us to weave the threads of your generous love
into the fiber of our beings and the activities of our daily lives.

Jean-Pierre Médaille's

The Maxims of the Little Institute

Suzanne Franck, CSJ

The Maxims of the Little Institute was written by a Jesuit priest, Father Jean-Pierre Médaille. These one hundred maxims were used to articulate the essence of the spirituality of the Sisters of St. Joseph. During the 17th century, few women received an education. Only two of the six founding Sisters of St. Joseph were able to read and write. With this in mind, Father Médaille developed one hundred maxims based on the values and virtues contained in the Gospels. From the first Sisters of St. Joseph and for many centuries, the maxims were memorized by the Sisters. Today, the maxims still provide a guiding foundation for Sisters and other people.

Father Médaille set the Sisters of St. Joseph on the Ignatian foundation of contemplation in action, a way of living that combines the mysticism of seeing God in all things with the practical response of being ready to do everything of which a woman is capable to serve God in the dear neighbor (McGlone 2017, 26). A few maxims have been selected for this publication. Read and reflect on the maxims for a deeper understanding of the charism of the Sisters of St. Joseph.

Explore the other maxims by visiting the US Federation of Sisters of St. Joseph's website at: https://www.cssjfed.org.

Prayer Using the Maxims

Author Unknown

O God,
Help us to undertake everything with great desire—
but remain hidden in carrying it out.

Teach us to be instruments of unity and reconciliation
for every kind of neighbor.

Fill us with a zeal that is contagious and
that multiplies women and men to be witnesses.

Push us to be bold and creative—
ready to risk going off the beaten path;
yet realistic at all times—
never neglecting common sense.

Let nothing stop us in works of mercy,
and may we do all these things
in humility and simplicity.

Maxim 2

Be perfected as God is perfect. Desire always to be who God created you to be.

Introduction

Only God is perfect—how can I be perfect? It is the ongoing journey of each moment unfolding within. To be "perfected" means I continue to strive to do my best and embrace, in all things, what brings about the greater glory of God.

Scripture

Philippians 3:13-15
John 4:34; 8:54

Reflection

Jesus is loving, forgiving, inclusive, and compassionate. Do these words describe me? What more is God asking of me?

Action

Step out of your comfort zone and do something that you feel God is calling you to do.

Maxim 8

Nothing is impossible for God. Have confidence and trust in God. Do everything for the glory of God through God's grace.

Introduction

Our world, filled with struggle and pain, needs to have hope. Our hope comes from our God through whom all things are possible. Trust in God's love for you and the grace of God working through you to bring God's presence to all.

Scripture

Matthew 14:22-23
1 Corinthians 16:13

Reflection

Do I believe that God loves me unconditionally just as I am? Do I trust in God, present and active in my ministry, my family, my friends, my daily life?

Action

Reach out to someone who is feeling overwhelmed or burdened with life, through a phone call, email, letter, or in person. Be the presence of God for them.

Maxim 11

Respect others and value highly the good in them. Walk with them and grow in justice and goodness together.

Introduction

All creation is interconnected and interdependent. My actions toward people and the rest of nature need to be respectful. Together we must grow in justice and goodness for the betterment of our world.

Scripture

Ephesians 4:32; 4:15
Revelation 16:24

Reflection

Do I value the gift of others and live with inclusive love?
How do I answer the question "Who is my neighbor?"

Action

Join with another person or group and support a justice issue—reach out to the marginalized or immigrant person.

Maxim 21

Desire neither praise nor reward for your good work in this life and you will have deeper and fuller life in eternity.

Introduction

God has created us uniquely and in God's image. I am called to live my life to the best of my ability and bring the Spirit of love and hope to all I meet and in all I do. I do this, not for the rewards it will bring, but rather because God dwells in me and I desire to be the goodness of God in the world.

Scripture

Matthew 6:3-4; 17-18
Philippians 2:6-8

Reflection

God uses me as an instrument of God's love. How have I been an instrument of God's love? To whom? Who has been a reflection of God's love in my life?

Action

Visit someone in the hospital or nursing home or donate time or a meal at a soup kitchen.

Maxim 52

Interpret all things from the best possible point of view.

Introduction

Is the cup half full or half empty? Is it partly sunny or partly cloudy? Trusting that God is within and around us, enter into each day and each moment with a positive and hopeful attitude.

Scripture

Matthew 7:1-5
Philippians 4:5
Mark 9:38-40

Reflection

Do I trust other people's goodness? Can I accept that others may be doing God's work even though their approaches are different from mine?

Action

Reflect on the blessings in your life. Make a list of all moments of gratitude in this day.

Maxim 64

Strive to be kind always to everyone and unkind to no one.

Introduction

The mission of the Sisters of St. Joseph is to welcome all people and all creation as "the dear neighbor." We have expanded our understanding to include not only people but all of God's creation, serving as stewards for God's precious gifts to us.

Scripture

Ephesians 4:2-4; 29-32
John 13:12-20
Romans 12:9-10; 14-18

Reflection

At the last supper, Jesus provided a profound example for us as he washed the feet of his disciples. Pope Francis has washed the feet of the prisoners and the homeless. Have I reached out to another with kindness, especially one that I find difficult?

Action

Do an act of kindness in a quiet way.

Maxim 73

Live out your life with one desire only: to be always what God wants you to be, in nature, grace and glory, for time and eternity.

Introduction

Each of us is created with unique gifts and a God-given purpose for our life. Reflect on the choices you make, listen to who and what God is calling you to be.

Scripture

Proverbs 16:1-3
Colossians 3:1-4
Philippians 2:6-11

Reflection

Do I accept the gift of who I am called to be by God?
How do I live this out?

Action

Celebrate your life today and the gifts that you are blessed with from God.

Closing Reflection

Bette Moslander, CSJ

Our zeal, like that of Jesus, will consume us if we are faithful. Like Jesus, rather than being drawn away from our suffering sisters and brothers, we will be poured out into the reality of the world. In that self-emptying, we will find ourselves in turn filled with the poor who suffer, the blind who cannot see, the imprisoned who struggle to be free, the oppressed who yearn for human rights, and the weepers who mourn in the anguish of the world. This is God incarnate within us. This God set us on fire with his or her own desire that all may be one. This desire for unity is the charism and its expression has as many facets as there are persons in the community. The Spirit invites us to read the signs of the times and interpret them in the light of the Gospel. Although the signs of our times are complex and often ambiguous, we must move with confidence among them. The Spirit demands that we integrate prayer and political action, prayer and social responsibility, prayer and peace, prayer and justice, and prayer and life. This integration is the contemplative action to which we are called.

We Walk in Communion

Shannon Green

Adapted from the prayer for the President's Inauguration,
Mount Saint Mary's University

God of love:

We walk in the company of our forbearers whose generous lives
have been given in service of the dear neighbor. You inspired them
to respond to the needs of their times, and so we now ask for their
prayers and guidance, as we seek to love without distinction.

The women of Le Puy, France, first Sisters of St. Joseph: Anna,
Clauda, Anna, Marguerite, Anna, and Françoise: you heard the
gospel and risked everything to respond to its call.

Jean-Pierre Médaille of the Society of Jesus: you placed your
education at the service of these women and in doing so empowered
them to find their own voices, visions and vocations.

Mother St. John Fontbonne: in the traumatic years following the
French Revolution, you regathered the scattered Sisters of St. Joseph
and under your leadership, the community began to thrive again
beyond all expectations.

You six sisters of Lyon who sailed across the Atlantic to Carondelet, Missouri: Delphine, Febronie, St. Protais, Marguerite-Félicité, Febronie and Philomène you responded to the needs of your times in a new land with resilience, humor, and tenacity.

You pioneer sisters who branched out across a young nation: you traveled to New York, Pennsylvania, Massachusetts, Minnesota, Louisiana, Illinois, California, Idaho, Washington, Canada, across North America to serve immigrant, the freed slave, the native communities, the poor and the disabled.

All you holy women and men, walk with us! Pray for us!

God eternal and ever-new, you pour out your Spirit upon every generation. Sustained by the gifts we have received from our founders, may we walk in your ways and live in your unifying love, striving always to move toward profound love of you, the dear neighbor, and all creation. Amen.

Acknowledgments

Martha Malinski, Executive Director
Association of Colleges of Sisters of St. Joseph

This publication would have never come to fruition without a core group of people. Special thanks to Lori Helfrich, who had an idea to compile a prayer book for use across member campuses. That idea sparked a working group that birthed and shaped this publication. Thanks to Carol Allan, SSJ (College of Our Lady of the Elms), Suzanne Franck, CSJ (St. Joseph's College), Shannon Green (Mount Saint Mary's University), Lori Helfrich (formerly with Fontbonne University), and Sean Peters, CSJ (The College of Saint Rose) for their hours of commitment and dedication to this project. This publication was truly a collaborative effort.

Two interns, Kalley Seeger, St. Catherine University, and Mary Sommerhauser, Avila University, also brought their skills to this project. The Association of Colleges of Sisters of St. Joseph is especially grateful to Mary Sommerhauser who brought her design talents, understanding and passion for the charism of the Sisters of St. Joseph and willingness to continue with the project long after the internship ended.

Thank you to the artists who allowed the Association of Colleges of Sisters of St. Joseph to use their work, especially Julie Lonneman, for her beautiful images of the first Sisters of St. Joseph who grace the cover and Mother St. John Fontbonne's image. Thank you to Carol Hebert, SSJ, whose illustration of the first kitchen transports us to Le Puy-en-Velay in 1650.

Thank you to all the writers who generously contributed: Carol Allan, SSJ, Pat Bergan, CSJ, Joannie Cassidy, SSJ, Jane DeLisle, CSJ, Suzanne Franck, CSJ, Joanne Gallagher, CSJ, Joan Marie Gleason, CSJ, Shannon Green, Kathleen Hanley, CSJ, Julie Harkins, CSJ, Lori Helfrich, Joan

Lescinski, CSJ, Joan Mitchell, CSJ, Bette Moslander, CSJ, Christine Parks, CSJ, Sean Peters, CSJ, Line Rioux, CSJ and the Sisters of St. Joseph in Lyon, Mary Sommerhauser, Kathy Sherman, CSJ, and Mary Catherine Walton, SSJ. A few of the authors are deceased. May they approve of how we have used their prayers to honor their lasting presence. Thank you to their congregations for granting permission to publish their work. For a few prayers and reflections, the working group was not able to identify authors for some of the well-loved and used reflections. Many thanks for their words.

The Association of Colleges of Sisters of St. Joseph's board of directors has been supportive of this project from the beginning. I want to express gratitude for their leadership at their institutions and in the Association for deepening the charism of the Sisters of St. Joseph. Thank you to Donald Boomgaarden (St. Joseph's College), Harry Dumay (College of Our Lady of the Elms), Antoinette Hays (Regis College), Ann McElaney-Johnson (Mount Saint Mary's University), Michael Pressimone (Fontbonne University), ReBecca Koenig Roloff (St. Catherine University), Ronald Slepitza (Avila University), Carolyn Stefanco (The College of Saint Rose) and Sister Carol Jean Vale (Chestnut Hill College).

Finally, thank you to all of the Sisters of St. Joseph who have walked before us, who walk with us now, and to those that will join us in the future. We are inspired, humbled and grateful for your commitment to the call of unifying love that unites neighbor with neighbor and neighbor with God without distinction. May this book serve as a resource and inspiration to integrate the charism on our campuses, in our lives, and in our community.

Resources for Deeper Understanding

Coburn, C. and Smith, M. *Spirited Lives: How Nuns Shaped Catholic Culture and American Life, 1836-1920*. Chapel Hill: The University of North Carolina Press, 1999.

McGlone, CSJ, Mary M. *Anything of Which Woman is Capable: A History of the Sisters of St. Joseph in the United States, Volume 1*. St. Louis: U.S. Federation of the Sisters of St. Joseph, 2017.

O'Marie, Carole. *Like a Swarm of Bees*. Graphic Vision. St. Paul: Good Ground Press, 2010.

Saravia, Maria. *In Spirit and Truth: Mother Saint John Fontbonne*. Lyon: Congregation of the Sisters of St. Joseph of Lyon, 2008.

Vacher, Marguerite. *Nuns without Cloister: Sisters of St. Joseph in the Seventeenth and Eighteenth Centuries*. (trans. P. Byrne). Lanham: University Press of America, Inc., 2010.

US Federation of the Sisters of St. Joseph, https://www.cssjfed.org